If a Tree Falls

THE GLOBAL IMPACT OF DEFORESTATION

NIKKI TATE

ORCA BOOK PUBLISHERS

Published in Canada and the United States in 2020 by Orca Book Publishers.
orcabook.com

Library and Archives Canada Cataloguing in Publication
Title: If a tree falls: the global impact of deforestation / Nikki Tate.
Names: Tate, Nikki, 1962– author.
Series: Orca footprints.
Description: Series statement: Orca footprints | Includes bibliographical references and index.
Identifiers: Canadiana (print) 20200186213 | Canadiana (ebook) 2020018623X | ISBN 9781459823556 (hardcover) | ISBN 9781459823563 (pdf) | ISBN 9781459823570 (epub)
Subjects: LCSH: Deforestation—Juvenile literature. | LCSH: Deforestation—Environmental aspects—Juvenile literature. | LCSH: Forests and forestry—Juvenile literature. | LCSH: Forests and forestry—Environmental aspects—Juvenile literature. | LCSH: Clearing of land—Juvenile literature. | LCSH: Clearing of land—Environmental aspects—Juvenile literature. | LCSH: Forest conservation—Juvenile literature.
Classification: LCC SD418 .T38 2020 | DDC j333.75/137—dc23

Library of Congress Control Number: 2020931819

Summary: Part of the nonfiction Orca Footprints series for middle readers and illustrated with color photographs. Find out how global deforestation affects the planet and what you can do to keep forests healthy for future generations.

Orca Book Publishers is committed to reducing the consumption of nonrenewable resources in the making of our books. We make every effort to use materials that support a sustainable future.

Orca Book Publishers gratefully acknowledges the support for its publishing programs provided by the following agencies: the Government of Canada, the Canada Council for the Arts and the Province of British Columbia through the BC Arts Council and the Book Publishing Tax Credit.

The authors and publisher have made every effort to ensure that the information in this book was correct at the time of publication. The authors and publisher do not assume any liability for any loss, damage, or disruption caused by errors or omissions. Every effort has been made to trace copyright holders and to obtain their permission for the use of copyrighted material. The publisher apologizes for any errors or omissions and would be grateful if notified of any corrections that should be incorporated in future reprints or editions of this book.

Design by Teresa Bubela
Layout by Dahlia Yuen
Front cover images by Mint Images/Getty Images and Hero Images/Getty Images
Back cover image by Somrerk Witthayanant/Shutterstock.com
Title page images by freepik.com and Julia Korchevska/Shutterstock.com
Author photo by Nigel Francis

Printed and bound in China.

23 22 21 20 • 1 2 3 4

My neighborhood in the Rocky Mountains would not be the same without the forests carpeting the lower flanks of the mountains.
ALEX WILLIAMS/UNSPLASH.COM

For Sarah Harvey, who has planted more seeds than she knows.

Contents

CHAPTER ONE
YOU CALL THAT A FOREST?

CHAPTER TWO
HOW WE HARVEST TREES

CHAPTER THREE
FORESTS OF TODAY

CHAPTER FOUR
TREES FOR THE FUTURE

Introduction

Many people (including me) feel a deep fondness for trees. There is something special about spending time in a forest.
CGN089/SHUTTERSTOCK.COM

Nearly 20 years ago I stood with a group of women in front of British Columbia's Parliament Buildings. As members of Women of the Woods, we were protesting our government's decision to cut down **old-growth forests** and export **raw logs**.

I was so concerned about what was going on in the forests close to my home that I wrote a novel called *Trouble on Tarragon Island*, about the struggle between the environmentalists who want to save trees and the logging industry that wants to cut them down.

The idea that we often make decisions based on how some people might benefit in the short term rather than on what's good for the planet and future generations has never made much sense to me.

Years later, when I was researching *Deep Roots: How Trees Sustain Our Planet*, I was reminded of just how much I love and appreciate trees. In that book I focused on different types of trees and what fascinating living beings they are.

TREE TRIVIA:
A dendrophile is someone who loves trees and forests.

I use products derived from forests every day, but the sight of a sea of stumps where a forest once stood makes my heart ache.
AURIMASM/DREAMSTIME.COM

Even though I love trees, I use the products they provide all the time. I'm working at a wooden desk in a house built of wood. There's nothing better than sitting in front of a fire when a blizzard howls outside. The book you are reading is printed on paper.

Though there has been progress when it comes to protecting the ancient forestland we have left, we are still figuring out the best ways to look after our forests while at the same time reaping the benefits trees provide.

In *If a Tree Falls* we will examine what makes forests such special and valuable **ecosystems** and why they are under threat. We'll also explore how people around the world are working together to make sure future generations can continue to enjoy the many ways forests help us live better lives.

CHAPTER ONE

You Call That a Forest?

WHAT IS A FOREST?

Unless you live in a desert or so far north that there are no trees at all, you have probably visited a forest, because trees grow in most parts of the world.

The definition of a forest is a "large area covered chiefly with trees and undergrowth." The kinds of plants and animals that live in the complex ecosystems within vary depending on where in the world the forest is found.

Some plant species thrive in the cool, moist shade provided by large old trees. If a windstorm blows through and knocks them down, this opens up the area for more sunlight, which allows different species to move in and flourish. Seeds sprout and young trees start growing.

Suzanne Simard is a professor of forest ecology who discovered that mother trees change their root structure to make room for baby trees, protecting them. Communicating through an underground web, or net, of *fungi*, mother trees send carbon and nitrogen to other trees who need it. When a mother tree is cut down, it affects all the plants and trees that are connected to it

Mangrove roots on the Aru Islands of Indonesia help prevent erosion. BIDOUZE/DREAMSTIME.COM

One of my favorite places to visit is Cathedral Grove on Vancouver Island. Young trees grow up through the fallen trunks of Douglas fir trees. NIKKI TATE

through the underground network. Young trees do not flourish when mother trees are removed.

In a replanted area the trees are generally of the same type and of a similar age, which creates very different types of ecosystems than you would find in a natural forest. Yes, these trees may grow fast and straight, but they do not recreate the structurally complex ecosystems of an old-growth forest. Old-growth forests include many different types of trees and other plants. They can't be easily replaced or regrown. Some of the trees are young and some are ancient, and this variety is what allows many different insects, birds and animals to thrive.

ADDING UP THE COSTS

Forests are more than just a bunch of trees. Not only are the world's forests home to 80 percent of the world's land animals and plants, but they also act as massive **carbon sinks**, helping to moderate climate change. Destroying forests disrupts the **water cycle.** This can happen locally and on a global scale. In certain areas forest loss may speed up desert formation. When forests

Mature forests include trees of all ages.
ROXANA GONZALEZ/DREAMSTIME.COM

The bark of this cedar tree has been stripped by Indigenous people on Vancouver Island. Trees like this are designated culturally modified trees. ANCIENT FOREST ALLIANCE

disappear, so too does a whole way of being for **Indigenous people** who have made their homes in the forest for generations. The relationship with the land impacts every aspect of Indigenous people's culture and knowledge.

TYPES OF FORESTS

Forests can be grouped into three main categories: tropical, temperate and boreal. The trees, plants and animals found in each type of forest change based on its distance north or south of the equator (latitude) and also on its **elevation**.

Tropical

Located close to the equator, tropical forests are wet and hot. The strong sun, stable temperatures and abundant rainfall enable these forests to support many different plant and animal species. Thick tree cover means that very little light penetrates the trees and reaches the forest floor, so only certain types of shade-loving plants survive at ground level. You may find as many as 1,500 flowering plants and 750 types of trees in a 4-square-mile (10-square-kilometer) area of tropical rainforest. In the wettest tropical rainforests the annual rainfall may be as much as 32 feet (10 meters)!

Children in Thailand play in the rainforest. SOMCHAI SANGUANKOTCHAKORN/DREAMSTIME.COM

My niece Zoe is dwarfed by this old Douglas fir tree in Cathedral Grove on Vancouver Island.
NIKKI TATE

From the Forest Floor

"To me forests were magical places, dark and safe yet mysterious and sometimes beautiful enough to invite silence and worship. Forests were places of wonder." —A.K. Hellum (author and forester)

Though I have often walked alone in forests, I never feel lonely among the trees.

If you have a forest you are able to visit, go and sit against a tree. Lean your head back and close your eyes. Breathe deeply. If you live in a city, this may be harder to do than if you live in (or are able to visit) a wild place, a forest. But even in cities, parks provide green spaces where it's possible to feel the special energy of trees.

If you've never spent much time in a forest, you might think that hanging out with trees would not be very interesting. But trust me—spend time in a forest and you won't think about trees in quite the same way again.

The leaves of many deciduous trees change color in the fall. DORIAN BAUMANN/UNSPLASH.COM

Temperate

Temperate forests are found in northeast Asia, western and central Europe, and parts of North America and New Zealand, all areas where there is a distinct winter. They are not as dense as tropical rainforests—some light reaches the ground—but the plants that grow under the trees must be able to tolerate shady conditions. Temperate forests include trees with broad leaves that change color each autumn, as well as **conifers**, whose leaves stay green year-round. Temperate forests may have only a dozen or so different tree species in a 4-square-mile (10-square-kilometer) area.

Boreal

Boreal forests are located between latitudes 50 and 60 degrees north. Most of them are found in Eurasia and North America. Long, cold, dry winters and a short growing season create a challenging growing environment. Most trees here are conifers such as pine, fir and spruce.

RAINFORESTS OF THE WORLD

It shouldn't surprise you that rainforests are wet—they aren't called desert forests, after all! But not all rainforests are hot and steamy. Though the most famous ones fall into the tropical category (like those found in the Amazon Basin in South America or the Congo Basin in Africa), rainforests are also located in other parts of the world.

Temperate rainforests, such as those found on British Columbia's west coast, are located in more northern latitudes. Cooler temperatures mean that humidity levels stay high.

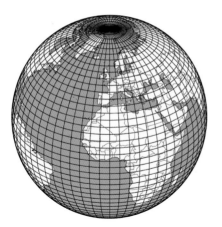

Imaginary lines running from pole to pole are called lines of longitude, or meridians. Lines running parallel to the equator are known as lines of latitude. This grid provides a handy way to identify any position on Earth. HELLERICK/WIKIPEDIA.ORG

TREE TRIVIA:
Most of the precipitation in a boreal forest falls as snow.

Vancouver Island forests are lush and green because of the abundant rainfall they receive each year. ROXANA GONZALEZ/DREAMSTIME.COM

In Victoria, British Columbia, where I lived for many years, the average rainfall is about 25 inches (635 millimeters) per year. The west coast of Vancouver Island, just a short distance away, sees even more rain. The town of Henderson Lake sometimes gets as much as 260 inches (6.6 meters) of rain in a year! That amount is taller than a very tall giraffe.

TOP TO BOTTOM

Different insects, birds, animals and other plant species are found in different types of forests. Forest life also changes depending on whether you are close to the ground or way up in the treetops. Forests have three or four levels.

Floor

Fallen leaves, sticks, branches, ripe fruit, dead trees and animal manure slowly rot to nourish and rebuild the soil.

Understory

Seedlings, saplings, shrubs and shade-loving plants grow close to the ground, where low levels of filtered sunlight are typical.

Canopy

This is the highest layer in a forest, where twigs, branches and leaves receive the most sun exposure.

Forests and the Air We Breathe

One of the reasons for protecting our remaining forests is the role trees play in producing oxygen. The air that we breathe contains about 20.9 percent oxygen. When we exhale we breathe out a waste product, carbon dioxide. Luckily for us, trees need carbon dioxide to grow. They breathe it in through their leaves, and when they exhale, trees produce oxygen as a by-product of *photosynthesis*. If we upset the balance and remove too many trees and plants from the planet, the health of the air we breathe suffers. Because of their central role in the circulation of carbon dioxide and oxygen, forests have been called the lungs of our planet.

The thick canopy in this Costa Rican rainforest creates lots of shade at ground level. JUHKU/DREAMSTIME.COM

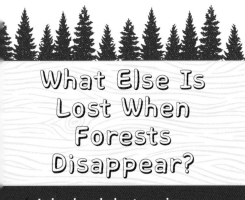

What Else Is Lost When Forests Disappear?

Animal and plant species are not the only things at risk when ecosystems are changed or destroyed. Approximately 2,000 Indigenous nations inhabited Brazil when European settlers first arrived in the sixteenth century, and now only about 200 remain. Deforestation and habitat destruction have contributed to the loss of their traditional languages, culture and knowledge of the region.

Emergent Layer

In tropical rainforests one or two individual trees will grow taller than the others. Seen from above, these giants poke up out of a sea of green.

ONE TREE, TWO TREES

How do we measure the health of our forests? One thing we look at is the size of the forest. One or two trees are not enough to function as a forest. The Food and Agriculture Organization of the United Nations (FAO) suggests forests need to be at least 1 acre (0.5 hectares) in size, with at least a 10 percent tree-canopy cover, to be able to sustain themselves. Trees in a healthy forest should be able to reach heights of at least 16 feet (5 meters). The amount of land covered by trees is one indication of how well we are doing with forest preservation.

BIRD'S-EYE VIEW

Between 2001 and 2017 about 883 million acres (337 million hectares) of tree cover was lost around the globe. That's larger than the land area of India. In a quarter of the locations, those trees probably won't ever grow back.

In other places, replanting is going on at a fast rate. Between 2001 and 2012, an estimated 199 million acres (80.6 million hectares) of trees were planted. We have the capacity to plant millions of trees, and it's encouraging that so many new trees are planted each year.

In countries such as Canada, where the government owns most of the forested land, logging companies are required by law to replant areas that have been logged.

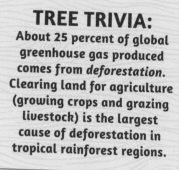

TREE TRIVIA:
About 25 percent of global greenhouse gas produced comes from *deforestation*. Clearing land for agriculture (growing crops and grazing livestock) is the largest cause of deforestation in tropical rainforest regions.

HOW OLD IS THAT FOREST?

We can also divide forests into categories based on how long they've been around and how they were established.

Old Growth

The trees and other plants found in old-growth forests are usually **native species**, those which would be found growing naturally in the area. These forests develop over hundreds, sometimes thousands, of years. Trees are of all ages and sizes. Trees in ancient forests eventually die of old age, at which point they fall, rot and provide new life to young seedlings and habitat for animals and other plants.

Secondary Growth

Secondary forests grow in areas where forests have been disturbed by logging or natural events such as windstorms or fires. Sometimes the area is allowed to regenerate naturally, and sometimes foresters replant. If many trees are planted at more or less the same time, secondary forests may be made up of trees that are close to the same age. Non-native species are more likely to invade and establish themselves in secondary-growth forests than in undisturbed forests.

In undisturbed forests, fallen trees rot where they lie, nourishing the soil. DAVE/UNSPLASH.COM

Neat rows of one species (like these oil palms in Malaysia) are typical of a plantation. RICH CAREY/SHUTTERSTOCK.COM

The red trees in the Helena National Forest in Montana have been killed by mountain pine beetles. FOREST SERVICE NORTHERN REGION/FLICKR.COM/CC BY 2.0

Plantations

Plantations are the most limited type of forest. They often feature a single type of tree, planted in rows, and there is little effort made to recreate a natural forest environment. Trees are treated like giant crops. Plantations often make use of fast-growing varieties because the trees will be recut as soon as possible. These trees generate the greatest amount of revenue in the least amount of time. This planting strategy is less supportive of **biodiversity.** If there's a lot of biodiversity in a forest, it's more likely that certain trees will be able to resist pests and disease or withstand environmental challenges like drought, climate change and pollution.

TIME FOR A CHECKUP!

When trees are stressed by drought, high temperatures or overcutting (which disrupts the ability of forests to regenerate themselves), their immune systems aren't as strong. It's more likely that weakened trees will die from disease, pests or damage due to fire or windstorms.

Measuring Forest Vital Signs

Scientists are able to measure chemical changes in plant cells that reflect plant stress levels. They can also measure how trees respond to factors like pollution and climate change by looking at growth ring patterns. Some scientists examine the fungal communities in soil to better understand how dead trees rot and become part of the soil.

Measuring the levels of different chemicals present in the soil and sharing that information with other experts makes it possible for scientists to find out how factors like air pollution are affecting forest health. For example, acid rain changes soil chemistry and makes it harder for trees to absorb water.

Forest Biodiversity

Forest biodiversity is another measure of how healthy and vibrant an ecosystem is. Some estimates put the number of species living in rainforests at 50 million. Many different kinds of plants, animals, birds and insects coexist in rainforests and rely on each other for survival.

Scientists in Australia studying cassowaries found that more than 150 different plants depend on these birds to spread their seeds. Without the birds to help plant the next generation, the trees and plants are also at risk.

Forest-dwelling cassowaries eat fallen fruit and distribute seeds with their poop.
LUC SESSELLE/DREAMSTIME.COM

HOW MUCH CARBON IS STORED IN FORESTS?

Forests remove carbon dioxide from the atmosphere during photosynthesis and act as carbon sinks by storing carbon dioxide in cell tissues. Both functions are believed to slow global warming. Scientists study ways to measure how much carbon is captured and stored in forested areas. Knowing exactly how much forests affect the balance of carbon dioxide in the atmosphere also helps us understand the extent to which they offset the negative impacts of climate change.

WHY DO FORESTS MATTER?

At the current rate of deforestation, some scientists estimate that the world's remaining rainforests will be gone within a hundred years.

What Is a Carbon Sink?

A natural environment that can absorb and store carbon—forest, ocean, peat bog or soil—is known as a carbon sink. Though you may hear a lot about how much carbon is captured and stored in tropical rainforests, on average temperate rainforests are even more effective as carbon sinks.

When Was the Industrial Revolution?

Between the second half of the eighteenth century and first part of the nineteenth, people began to use machines to do a lot of the work formerly done by human and animal labor. Those machines need a source of power to operate. Gasoline, diesel, coal and wood are some examples of fuels burned to generate power.

Trees and Climate Change

The vast majority of scientists agree that average global temperature increases have caused (and will continue to cause) a wide range of changes on Earth. These changes include melting ice at the poles, more severe and unpredictable storms, flooding in some areas and droughts in others.

If the world is trying to avoid global warming of more than 1.5°C (2.7°F) above preindustrial temperatures, forests could play a key role by absorbing large amounts of the carbon dioxide produced by burning fossil fuels (coal, oil and gas).

Pollution from factories, power plants, cars and the burning of wood and bushes to clear land for agriculture are some sources of the carbon dioxide that contributes to climate change. Forests and vegetation absorb about 25 percent of the carbon dioxide that humans pump into the atmosphere through their activities, which is why many people believe that protecting forests (and planting more trees) is so important.

Factories, mills and agriculture contribute to pollution and increased levels of carbon dioxide in the atmosphere.
ALEXANDER OGANEZOV/DREAMSTIME.COM

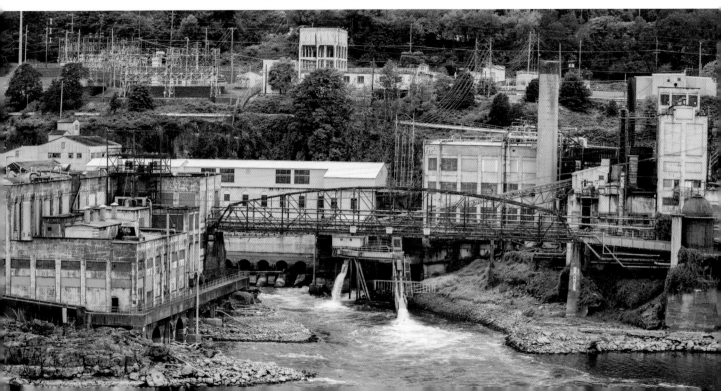

Forests and the Water Cycle

When trees "exhale" through their leaves, water evaporates. This process is called *transpiration*. When enough trees send water into the atmosphere, clouds form. Eventually the water droplets fall back down to Earth's surface.

Removing forests on a large scale results in a decrease in rainfall and, in extreme cases, devastating droughts. Ironically, clearing trees to make room for crops can backfire, as crops don't grow well in drought conditions.

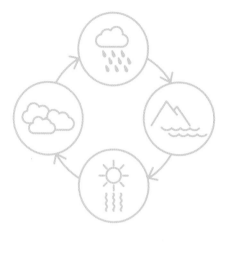

Forests and Floods

Soil **erosion** is a serious global issue. When we clear the trees from a large area of land, the soil is no longer protected from the sun and wind. Without the web of tree roots helping to hold the soil in place, floods can wash away that precious top layer of soil needed to grow crops or more trees.

New Medicines from Rainforests

When local Indigenous people are forced to leave their traditional homes after forests are cut down (often by non-Indigenous people), their knowledge of plants used for medicine or food is often lost along with the plants. It's estimated that about 7,000 active medication ingredients were originally found in plants, many of which grow in tropical rainforests. These include drugs used to treat infections, heart disease, depression and other illnesses.

In 2018, researchers exploring a remote inland temperate rainforest in British Columbia (in the Ancient Forest/Chun T'oh Whudujut Provincial Park) identified 2,400 species of plants, some newly discovered.

It's impossible to predict how many future discoveries we may miss out on if our remaining rainforests are destroyed.

Drugs derived from the rose periwinkle (Catharanthus roseus) have been used to treat cancer. RAMESHNG/WIKIMEDIA.ORG

CHAPTER TWO

How We Harvest Trees

The world's population is just over 7.7 billion people. Every day, land is cleared for farms and to build new cities, towns and roads. Trees are valuable as a source of building materials and for fuel.

In 2017 the forest industry in Canada generated about $24.6 billion and employed more than 200,000 people. Countries like Canada, the United States, Finland, Russia, Germany and Sweden all produce large volumes of forest products each year. We use wood and wood products for everything from chopsticks and homes to paper and cardboard to fuel for cooking and heat.

There is no reason to think our demand for timber is going to slow down anytime soon. With so many jobs at stake and so much money being generated by the forest industry, companies will continue to look at forests in terms of how much wood they will be able to harvest and sell.

Finding a balance between cutting trees down and preserving them as forests is tricky. Understanding why we make the decisions we do about forest management begins by looking at our history with the woods.

In September 2010, marchers in South Kalimantan in Indonesia gathered to protest palm oil plantations.
IMAN SATRIA/SHUTTERSTOCK.COM

Traditional knowledge of foods, plants and medicines is often lost when forests disappear. SJORS737/DREAMSTIME.COM

HAVE WE EVER BEEN KIND TO OUR FORESTS?

People and forests have always been closely connected. Forests provide food, medicine, shelter and fuel, and in days gone by people's lives were closely linked to the forest ecosystems. In a few isolated places (in the Amazon Basin, for example), a handful of people still live in much the same way as they have for many generations.

Researchers have found that ancient peoples all over the world have changed forest ecosystems through the burning, selective harvesting and cultivation of plants.

In Oregon, before European settlers arrived, deliberately set fires mimicked the natural burning cycle of wildfires. These fires cleared out dense underbrush and allowed saplings of sun-loving species to grow. The more open terrain made it easier for people to hunt game as large as deer and as small as grass-hoppers. The fires were set at the end of the summer, after berries and nuts had been harvested and stored.

Major Causes of Deforestation

1. **Agriculture:** crops
2. **Agriculture:** grazing land
3. **Forestry:** building material
4. **Forestry:** pulp and paper
5. **Fuel:** cooking fires
6. **Fuel:** heat

Studies of burnt forests reveal that some species, such as the black-backed woodpecker, thrive in this unique ecosystem. These birds love to nest in the blackened tree trunks after a fire has moved through an area. KURT BAUSCHARDT/FLICKR.COM

Can Fire Be a Good Thing?

Images of raging, out-of-control fires are shocking, but some ecosystems depend on occasional fires to stay healthy. Lodgepole pine seeds germinate *only* after a fire has passed through. Until intense heat melts the resin that seals the seeds inside lodgepole cones, the seeds are trapped. Only after a fire do these seeds come in contact with the soil and moisture they need to begin to sprout.

Some trees have built-in recovery systems to help them bounce back quickly after being damaged by fire.

ELANTSEV/DREAMSTIME.COM

If fire is a natural way for forests to renew themselves, we should think more about protecting homes and communities located close to wild areas and less about preventing wildfires in wilderness areas. People love to build near the woods, but they need to leave space between the edge of the forest and vulnerable homes. Other precautions include clearing underbrush close to buildings and removing dead pine needles from gutters.

THE INDUSTRIAL ERA

When European settlers migrated to the Americas, they brought along their own ideas of how land and forests should be used. The new arrivals cleared away trees to make space for settlements.

They also recognized forests as a source of wood products to be sold. Timber barons made fortunes cutting down trees and turning those trees into planks and boards for use in construction, sometimes far from the forest where the trees were cut down.

Indigenous Peoples have a relationship with the land that relies on the balanced use of available resources (including forests). European settlers, on the other hand, thought of the forests as possessions to be managed, sold, manipulated and stripped. Replanting was done only so the cycle could be repeated. These attitudes still dominate many people's ideas of how forests should be used today.

A GROWING APPETITE

Railways and roads connected communities across North America as settlers moved west in the nineteenth and early twentieth centuries. Heavy machinery changed the way people worked the land and harvested trees. Pressure on larger areas of forest increased when it wasn't just local farmers clearing areas for agriculture, but also forestry companies feeding the world's growing appetite for lumber and wood products.

Many floating logs gathered together for transport by water are called a log boom.
LENNART HEIM/UNSPLASH.COM

COMMON LOGGING METHODS

Most of the trees harvested in the forests of North America are removed in a process called clear-cutting. In a clear-cut every tree in the logging area is cut down. The best trees (those large and straight enough to be valuable as lumber or that are the right type for pulp and paper) are removed from the site. The remaining waste (woody material, branches, undersized stems, and tree-tops) is often stacked and burned before the area is replanted.

TREE TRIVIA:
Screening clear-cuts from public view is common practice in British Columbia, where a band of green trees is often left along the highway. You don't have to go far from the road to see land beyond the green belt that has been completely cleared.

From the Forest Floor

In northern hemisphere countries, forest fires are destroying larger and larger areas of forest each year. Warmer average temperatures mean hotter, drier summers. Places like the United States, Canada and Sweden struggle to stay ahead of massive fires.

For the past several summers I've watched the mountains that surround me disappear in a thick haze of yellow smoke from forest fires burning in western North America. Though some of these fires are caused by careless humans, others are started by lightning strikes. It can be hard to detect fires that begin in remote areas. If these fires are difficult to get to, it's almost impossible to mount an effective firefighting effort. My normally healthy mountain air becomes a toxic cloud. The air quality can be so poor that spending the day outside is just as bad for my lungs as if I had smoked 10 cigarettes.

In a clear-cut forest like this one almost every tree is cut down. SAM BEEBE/FLICKR.COM

Selective Logging

If only certain trees are removed while others remain standing, we say a forest has been selectively logged. Leaving some trees in place is said to be less harmful than clear-cutting. Some researchers are concerned that even removing a few trees can lead to changes in the forest environment.

There is no rule that says exactly how many trees can be removed when an area is selectively logged. That means sometimes more trees are removed than can reasonably be expected to regenerate.

Checkerboard Forests

Smaller *cutblocks* arranged in a checkerboard pattern may help with wildlife management and reduce some of the environmental impacts of clear-cutting. How effective the strategy is depends on the size of the cutblock, the terrain and how the blocks are arranged.

Checkerboard cutblocks were not originally established for environmental reasons. When the Oregon and California Railroad needed access to land between the two states to build the railway in the 1860s, the federal and local governments divided up the forestland in alternating blocks to better distribute tax revenues earned from timber cutting.

These days, cutblocks tend to be smaller and irregularly shaped rather than square. Foresters design them to follow natural land contours, and consider streams and rivers in order to try to protect some habitat for wildlife. This strategy also encourages some natural seeding in cleared areas.

What Is Stumpage?

In British Columbia, logging companies manage government-owned forests. The companies pay for building roads and logging, hauling and processing the trees. Rather than paying to rent the land, tree-felling costs and an agreed-upon profit amount are subtracted from what the companies can make by selling wood products. The amount that's left over is called stumpage and is paid to the government. The exact way stumpage is calculated varies from place to place.

When viewed from space, the checkerboard pattern of forest cutblocks in Idaho and Montana is quite obvious. NASA/GSFC/METI/ERSDAC/JAROS AND U.S./JAPAN ASTER SCIENCE TEAM

Rev It Up!

One of the tools used in the logging industry is the chainsaw, a mechanical saw with sharp cutting teeth attached to a continuous chain.

The earliest chainsaws were invented by doctors in the late 1700s who needed a way to cut through bone. In 1905 the first patent for a chainsaw was given to Samuel J. Bens, who planned to use his invention to fell redwood trees in California. By the 1930s gasoline-powered portable chainsaws were being produced by several companies. The early models were so heavy and awkward, it took two men to operate them.

In the 1950s advances in technology and the creation of lighter materials led to chainsaws a person could use alone. Having a portable, powerful tool that allowed one person to cut down trees, remove branches and trim logs to size changed the forest industry forever.

Today chainsaws are most likely to be used on steep slopes that are hard to access with large equipment. The trend in commercial forestry is to use larger, more efficient equipment and fewer people to harvest trees faster.

Forestry workers use chainsaws light enough for one person to handle but powerful enough to cut through large trees and thick branches.
ROBERTAX/DREAMSTIME.COM

THE MODERN FOREST INDUSTRY

In the United States, trees that are grown on public lands are sold to large timber corporations. The roads used to haul the cut trees from the forests are often paid for by taxes collected collected from citizens. Roads built to access remote areas allow large logging trucks to remove massive piles of logs at one time. Trees are cut down and then moved to areas where trucks can be loaded.

Getting the Logs Out

Logs are dragged, or skidded, from where the tree is cut to the loading point. To get them there, sometimes systems of cables are used to send cut logs soaring down steep hillsides.

TREE TRIVIA:
Misery whip is a slang term for a two-man crosscut saw with a single blade and a handle at each end.

GERALD W. WILLIAMS COLLECTION/OREGON STATE UNIVERSITY SPECIAL COLLECTIONS AND ARCHIVES

Other Ways of Harvesting Wood

In Great Britain in the Middle Ages, certain types of trees (such as willows, oaks and maples) were coppiced on a strict schedule. Coppicing is the practice of cutting down a tree and allowing shoots to grow from the stump left behind.

By coppicing the same fast-growing trees every seven years, foresters were guaranteed a steady supply of long, straight rods and sticks. These sticks were used as fuel; for building houses, animal shelters and fences; and as supports for vines. Many were used by local farmers and villagers, but plenty were also shipped overseas.

This rocking chair is made from supple twigs. DADEROT/WIKIMEDIA.ORG

Logs are then moved to mills, where they are processed for use in construction, manufacturing or the pulp and paper industry. In some cases, these raw logs are shipped to other countries for processing.

Some of the world's most valuable trees are found in ancient forests. Mature slow-growing trees such as cedar are particularly valuable because they produce strong wood that's less likely to warp over time. Because this kind of wood is in such high demand, tree poachers sometimes sneak into protected areas to illegally cut trees down and sell them. Some of these trees grow in remote places where there are few official patrols. Poachers know it's unlikely they will be caught and prosecuted for breaking the laws designed to protect big old trees.

FORESTS FOR RENT

In Canada the government grants forest licenses to companies, giving them the right to harvest trees in particular areas. The maximum length of a license is 20 years. Companies with a forest license are responsible for forest management, road-building and reforestation.

NOT JUST FALLING TREES

While chopping down trees has an obvious impact on a forest, logging affects forests in other ways too. Logging roads split one large forest into several smaller ones. The roads provide pathways for non-native species to enter. Roads also create new forest edges with microhabitats that are different from those of the forest interior.

THE NEED FOR SPEED

Modern machinery means we are able to alter the landscape quickly and on a massive scale, but should we?

Large-scale forestry businesses harvest trees for financial profit. Governments often find it hard to balance the need to protect forested lands on behalf of citizens against the need to generate revenue paid by logging companies for the right to harvest trees from public lands. The short-term financial gain may outweigh the long-term environmental benefits of leaving large areas of forestland intact. There is a lot of debate in the logging industry and among environmentalists, scientists and government officials about how many trees need to be replanted and how forests should be managed to ensure there will be healthy forests for future generations.

Modern equipment speeds up the process of harvesting trees. KLETR/SHUTTERSTOCK.COM

Logging trucks like this one are a common sight in places with an active forest industry, such as British Columbia.
STOCKSTUDIOX/GETTY IMAGES

CHAPTER THREE

Forests of Today

The Great Bear Rainforest is located on British Columbia's Pacific coast and is part of the Pacific temperate rainforest ecoregion. The Great Bear Rainforest covers about 12,000 square miles (32,000 square kilometers) and is one of the largest unspoiled areas of temperate rainforest on Earth. JACK BORNO/CC BY-SA 3.0

Planting trees in previously forested areas (reforestation) and adding tree coverage to new areas (*afforestation*) are both pro-forest solutions to the problem of deforestation. Another strategy is to protect and preserve the old-growth forest ecosystems we have left.

The well-being of our forests affects everyone. That's true whether we live at the edge of a forest, above the arctic circle or in the heart of a big city. International trade has connected our world in ways we could not have imagined a few hundred years ago. Decisions made about forest management on one side of the world can have an impact on climate and the availability of food and building supplies thousands of miles away.

FORESTS, FOOD AND FARMING

In areas like Costa Rica, where large amounts of land are owned or controlled by banana producers, it's difficult for the local people to grow food for themselves. If priority were given to local farmers on smaller plots meeting their own food needs, less land would have to be cleared, and the remaining forests would have a better chance of survival.

Going Bananas

In 1950 about 90 percent of the land in the Sarapiquí Valley in Costa Rica was covered with rainforest. By 2005, only about 25 percent remained. Of that land area, just a small amount is fully protected in biological reserves.

Even though the banana industry in Costa Rica is responsible for the loss of a lot of rainforest (and the plant and animal species that live there), it still has a lot of support. Banana plantations hire workers who, in turn, support small local businesses. The banana companies pay taxes, and this helps local communities build **infrastructure** like schools, roads and hospitals. The Costa Rican government benefits from tax revenues, which help pay for the debt owed to other governments and international banks. Other types of agriculture (raising cattle on land cleared for grazing and producing coffee, chocolate or palm oil) are also major contributors to tropical rainforest losses.

Do Nothing—A Park Creates Itself

Pacific Spirit Regional Park in Vancouver is 1,885 acres (763 hectares) of forest that is much loved and appreciated by the many people who visit it or live close by. The forest is lush, with a mixture of tree species (cedar, Douglas fir, western hemlock, alder, maple and cherry). Even though it looks as if the forest has been there for a very long time, this area was clear-cut in 1914. Left alone, the forest regenerated without any special intervention by people.

In his book *Green Spirit: Trees Are the Answer,* author Patrick Moore reminds us that even the most decimated areas can regenerate if given enough time. Now protected, Pacific Spirit Park gives thousands of people each year the chance to spend time in a lush temperate rainforest located just minutes from a bustling city.

Banana plantations such as this one in Nicaragua look nothing like the rainforests they replace. MATTMCINNIS/DREAMSTIME.COM

Food for Families

After years of growing and harvesting bananas, Costa Rican banana plantations eventually strip the soil of many important nutrients. This means fewer bananas are produced. Sometimes companies abandon plantations that are not profitable enough. Local families then try to establish small farms to grow food for themselves. It's hard to grow enough food to support a family, especially when the soil quality is poor.

A similar situation occurs with other cash crops like coffee, chocolate and palm oil.

Digging Deep

Rainforest soils are not particularly fertile once they are stripped of the original trees and plants that lived there, so companies wanting to maximize production often use chemical fertilizers and pesticides. These chemicals leech out of the soil when it rains and may run off into local freshwater streams and rivers. This in turn can increase algae growth in rivers to a point where animals that eat algae can't eat all of it. The excess algae dies and begins to decompose with the help of bacteria. These bacteria use so much oxygen, there isn't enough left in the water for other aquatic life, such as fish.

When too much oxygen is removed from water, there may not be enough left to sustain fish and other aquatic life.
GERALD MARELLA/DREAMSTIME.COM

PALM OIL PLANTATIONS

Palm oil is used in such products as margarine, shampoo, chocolate and biodiesel. Companies that establish palm oil plantations clear large areas of rainforest land, sometimes illegally (without a license).

Indonesia is a country that produces a lot of palm oil. Oil palms grow well on cleared land that was once tropical rainforest. Because some trees are cut illegally, it can be difficult to know exactly how much forest is being lost each year.

Protests, petitions and media appearances all contributed to raising awareness about the environmental impacts of palm oil plantations. COURTESY OF RAINFOREST ACTION NETWORK

There are laws in place in Indonesia aimed at preventing companies from removing rainforests. Corruption, lack of enforcement and inaccurate reporting mean the laws have not been as effective as hoped, and protection of the remaining rainforest is happening slowly.

Governments elsewhere in the world are restricting imports of biodiesel fuel made from palm oil, and this may lower the value of palm oil and discourage additional clearing.

WHERE DO YOUR COOKIES COME FROM?

A snack in your lunchbox may have started out thousands of miles from where you live. Reading the labels on packaged foods is one way to get an idea of what's in your food, and from there online research can tell you a lot about the origins of those ingredients.

In 2007, 11-year-old Girl Scouts Rhiannon Tomtishen and Madison Vorva from Ann Arbor, Michigan, made the connection between forest habitat destruction, orangutan deaths and the palm oil contained in Girl Scout cookies. In places like Indonesia, orangutans rely on rainforest habitat for food and shelter.

Habitat destruction in the rainforests of eastern Madagascar has pushed this species of lemur to the brink of extinction. TOM JUNEK/ CC BY-SA 3.0

Orangutans in Indonesia need intact rainforests to survive in the wild. YUSNIZAM YUSOF/SHUTTERSTOCK.COM

After the girls did a science-fair presentation about rainforests, they refused to sell Girl Scout cookies and began a campaign to change the ingredients used in the cookies. They wrote letters, gathered signatures on a petition and encouraged other Girl Scouts to take up the cause. They traveled to New York to speak with representatives of the Girl Scouts organization. Finally the organization agreed to work with cookie manufacturers to make sure that palm oil used in the cookies did not come from sources causing further deforestation.

The Kellogg Company (responsible for making the Girl Scout cookies at the time) announced it would only use palm oil produced on environmentally responsible plantations.

Today Girl Scout cookies are made by bakers who are members of the Roundtable on Sustainable Palm Oil (RSPO). This organization includes palm oil farmers and manufacturers as well as conservationists.

THE AMAZON BASIN

Since about 1970 almost 310,000 square miles (800,000 square kilometers) of rainforest in the Amazon Basin in Brazil have been cut down. That's bigger than Michigan, Wisconsin, Illinois, Indiana and Ohio put together!

Though forests everywhere are being cut, tropical rainforests like those in Brazil have been hit particularly hard.

TREE TRIVIA:
Each year approximately 20 billion pairs of disposable wooden chopsticks, made from such woods as aspen, willow or birch, are used in Japan. Chopsticks made of bamboo fiber come from Malaysia, Indonesia and China.

For a time fewer trees were being cut down in the Amazon, but recent changes in government policy have allowed an increase in the rate of forest destruction. The majority of the land is being used for agriculture, urban expansion and industry. Only about 20 percent of previously forested land in the country is regrowing forest.

RAINFORESTS IN THE CONGO BASIN

The second-largest area of rainforest after the Amazon Basin is in central Africa in the Congo Basin. The World Wildlife Fund estimates that about 75 million people live in an area that covers about 500 million acres (202 million hectares). Many residents rely on the forest for their survival. This area is also home to forest elephants, gorillas, chimpanzees, bonobos and more than 400 other species of animals.

When compared to some other rainforest regions, the Congo Basin still has a large area of surviving rainforest. Various organizations and foreign governments recognize the value of these large forests, the diversity of species that live there and the role of large, intact forest tracts when it comes to moderating climate change. Because some countries in this region are not wealthy, payments have been made to regional governments to help with forest preservation.

THE WORLD'S HUNGER FOR PAPER

A third of the wood exported from rainforests each year is turned into paper. The Indonesian island of Sumatra, the sixth-largest in the world, is a source of a lot of that paper. Until the end of the nineteenth century, most of Sumatra was covered in lush rainforest. Orangutans, elephants and tigers lived in this rich ecosystem, along with many other species of plants, animals, insects and birds.

The northern spotted owl lives in old-growth forests in the Pacific Northwest. Nesting pairs do not like to relocate, and their numbers have declined drastically as old-growth forests have disappeared. REESE FERRIER/DREAMSTIME.COM

What Can We Do?

Paper and paper products can and should be recycled. Make an effort to keep paper and cardboard out of the landfill. When purchasing paper products (from toilet paper and paper towels to notebooks and postcards), see if the item has been made with recycled paper. Try to buy items with as little packaging as possible and consider reusable (or recycled) wrapping paper for gifts.

Forest loss in Sumatra has been hard on elephants. Land continues to be cleared to make room for new palm oil plantations.
DIKKY OESIN/SHUTTERSTOCK.COM

In the twentieth century more people moved to the island, and timber companies set their sights on the rainforests. Today only about 3 percent of the original rainforest remains. Hardwood trees such as teak and mahogany were logged for export, and while they may have been the first victims of the government-approved logging frenzy, other species of trees have been cut too in order to satisfy the world's desire for paper. Once rainforest land has been cleared, fast-growing species like acacia and eucalyptus are often planted. These trees can be harvested for processing at pulp and paper mills in as little as six to eight years.

Animals in Danger in Sumatra

The Sumatran tiger is the smallest in the world. Males weigh from 220 to 310 pounds (100 to 140 kilograms). According to Tigers in Crisis, only 400 to 600 Sumatran tigers remain. The species is critically endangered. The Sumatran Asian elephant also lives on the island and, like the tiger, is facing increasing pressures from deforestation, poaching and conflicts with people competing for scarce land resources. There are only about 2,000 left.

Working Together

The only way to help ensure the future of the species that live in places like Indonesia is to protect the habitat that supports them. This is true in forests elsewhere in the world.

Children in a Brazilian village enjoy climbing trees. SJORS737/DREAMSTIME.COM

In 2012 the Dansk Ornithologisk Forening/BirdLife Denmark), the Royal Society for the Protection of Birds (based in the UK), BirdLife International and Burung Indonesia pooled their resources to gain control over an area of lowland rainforest in Sumatra. The 100-year agreement should protect the Harapan Rainforest and land that supports almost 300 bird species as well as tigers and elephants. Working closely with local people who have always lived in the forest, the group hopes to see this area recover from previous forestry activity and become an example for how natural areas of forests can be managed in other places.

THE POWER OF TREES

The need to create electric power for homes, factories, hospitals, businesses and schools also contributes to deforestation. As of 2011, 3,500 billion kilowatt-hours of energy (that's about 16 percent of all the world's power) came from hydroelectric sources. Most of this power comes from 45,000 dams located in 160 countries. By building a dam, the greatest amount of reliable power can be generated from a river. However, this also means flooding large areas of land to create a reservoir.

The Barrier Dam on the Kananaskis River produces about 40,000 megawatt hours of power each year. C. OLSON/ALBERTA WILDERNESS ASSOCIATION

From the Forest Floor

Not far from where I live, several dams were built, starting in the 1930s. The dams that control water flow on the Kananaskis River and Kananaskis Lakes have changed the landscape in the area. Once famous for its forested islands, this area is now a large body of water. One of the things I try to do is reduce my use of electricity by turning off the lights and unplugging electronics I'm not using. If we all do this, we can help our existing power sources go further and perhaps delay or eliminate the need for new dams.

CHAPTER FOUR

Trees for the Future

Sometimes change begins with ordinary citizens. In other cases, governments implement new laws to create change.

STANDING TALL FOR TREES

In British Columbia, logging companies continue to cut down trees in some of the few remaining stands of old-growth temperate forest and ship raw logs offshore for processing, even though many citizens oppose these practices.

But citizen pressure can be an effective way to alter government policy, even if change comes about slowly. In the early 1990s protesters on Vancouver Island's west coast blocked logging roads in massive peaceful protests in the Clayoquot Sound area. Nine hundred protesters were arrested in what is still the largest act of *civil disobedience* in Canadian history. The end result was protection for some of the world's most valuable old-growth forests.

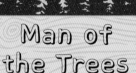

Man of the Trees

One of the world's first global conservationists was Richard St. Barbe Baker, sometimes known as the Man of the Trees. Many people were influenced by St. Barbe Baker's work, and some of the world's largest reforestation projects can be traced back to his early efforts in the twentieth century.

Hundreds of people were arrested for blocking logging roads in an effort to protect the old-growth forests of Clayoquot Sound.

RICK EGLINTON/TORONTO STAR PHOTOGRAPH ARCHIVE, COURTESY OF TORONTO PUBLIC LIBRARY

However, there is still lots of work to be done. According to the Sierra Club, Vancouver Island's remaining old-growth forests are still being cut at a rate of about 43 football fields each day.

THE GREAT GREEN WALL

In 1954 Richard St. Barbe Baker suggested planting a broad band of trees to slow the spread of the Sahara Desert. In 2002, on the World Day to Combat Desertification and Drought, regional leaders reconsidered his idea. The Great Green Wall project has since brought together more than 20 African nations in an effort to plant a green belt of trees across sub-Saharan Africa to try to stop the advancing desert. When complete, the planned strip will be almost 5,000 miles (8,000 kilometers) long and 9 miles (15 kilometers) wide.

TREE TRIVIA:
A eucalyptus tree can reach harvestable size in six to eight years.

Eucalyptus trees are native to Australia. Their leaves provide food for koala bears.

RENNETT STOWE/FLICKR.COM/CC BY 2.0

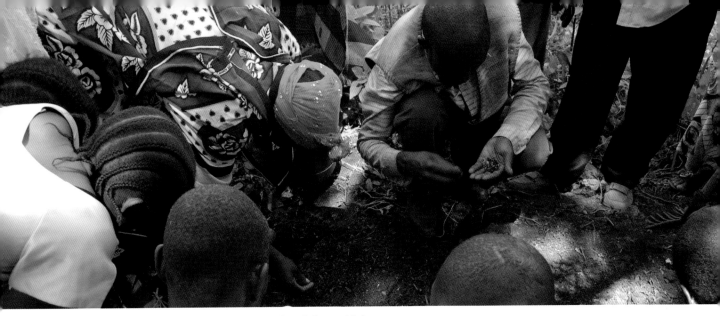

Villagers in Tanzania work together to sort seeds to help establish a tree nursery. TREES FOR THE FUTURE/FLICKR.COM/CC BY 2.0

A Few of the World's Most Gorgeous Forests

Whether you travel and visit these forests in person or check them out online, they are destinations worth seeing!

The Daintree Rainforest in Australia is part of the Wet Tropics of Queensland and is thought to be one of the oldest rainforests on Earth.

Monteverde Cloud Forest Biological Reserve in Costa Rica is home to spiny rats, toucans and tapirs.

If you are looking for giant pandas or Sichuan golden snub-nosed monkeys, then the Jiuzhai Valley National Park (also known as Jiuzhaigou), Sichuan, China, is the place to go.

WHAT GOVERNMENTS CAN DO

Individual governments have also seen opportunities to change the way they treat forests. Reforestation in South Korea began in the 1950s after the country was stripped of trees as the result of war and occupation, when trees were cut for fuel and to make wood products. Because of changes in government policy in the 1950s, today about two-thirds of the country is once again forested.

In Tanzania, tree ownership certificates were part of a unique strategy to encourage a sense of responsibility and stewardship for some of the 6.4 million trees planted over the course of a nine-year reforestation project started in 1990. Because Tanzanian law did not allow women to own land, the system of tree certificates made it possible for women to own and control what would become a valuable resource. The trees were owned by individuals regardless of who owned the land where the trees grew.

The original planting project expanded to more villages, and providing young trees to plant has become an excellent small business venture as the seedlings and young trees are sold to other nearby villages.

INTRODUCING EXOTIC SPECIES

Sometimes people plant species of trees that don't naturally grow in an area. If the introduced species thrive and grow too quickly, they can push out native species, sometimes to the point where local plants or animals become rare or even extinct. It is hard to predict the impact a non-native species will have on the local ecosystem. Many governments restrict the movement of seeds and plants from one area to another for this reason. In British Columbia, for example, foresters must use approved seeds that are appropriate for the site being replanted.

These mud balls contain tree seeds used for afforestation projects.
AMRITANSHU SINGH/DREAMSTIME.COM

CHINA

Because of China's need for fuel, building materials and land for farming, large areas of forests were cleared before the 1990s.

Without trees, land was particularly vulnerable to flooding. After massive flooding of the Yangtze River in 1998, China's government banned logging in natural forests. At the end of the 1990s the Chinese government got serious about afforestation efforts. Planting trees has been identified as an important way to protect topsoil, prevent flooding and fight global warming.

As of 2013, about 69 million acres (27.9 million hectares) of forests have been replanted in 26 different Chinese provinces. That represents a land area about the size of Denmark. It's hoped that 35 billion trees will have been planted in northern China by 2050.

The downside of this type of afforestation is that China's new forests rely on a few varieties of fast-growing trees, and the young trees need a lot of water. Scientists are worried that the thirsty saplings will use up too much of the available ***groundwater.***

TREE TRIVIA:
Aggressive planting projects mean that China now has the largest human-made forest in the world.

March 12 is National Tree Planting Day in China. Many countries, states and cities set aside a special day each year to recognize the importance of trees. This celebration is often known as Arbor Day. DONKEYRU/DREAMSTIME.COM

From the Forest Floor

My step-grandfather was a woodworker in Germany. One of Opa's responsibilities was to manage a small forest that had been owned by the family for generations.

The oldest, healthiest trees were never cut down, as they produced the best seeds for the next generation of trees. Opa thinned areas of the forest that became too thick and overgrown. Selecting certain trees for cutting allowed more light to reach the forest floor, and this encouraged seedlings and saplings (young trees) to grow more quickly.

Opa was careful not to cut down more trees than could grow back. There were no large holes in the forest, as only a few trees were taken down each year.

Merv Wilkinson began a sustainable logging practice on 77 acres (31 hectares) of land known as Wildwood, on Vancouver Island, in 1945. For years he supported his family by carefully harvesting selected trees. The land is now owned and protected by the Ecoforestry Institute Society.

THE LAND CONSERVANCY OF BRITISH COLUMBIA

CHANGES IN BEHAVIOR BEGIN WITH CHANGES IN ATTITUDE

How can we shift old ways of thinking and reconsider our role on the planet as caretakers as well as consumers?

In many places in the world, large areas of land are owned by the government. Some of this land is set aside as parkland for all citizens to enjoy. Sometimes governments allow corporations to use public lands in order to access valuable resources found there. Mines and forestry operations may be located on land owned by the government. Sometimes corporations and governments work together and share profits from selling natural resources.

A healthy environment and preserving wild places for future generations are goals that a government may choose to make a priority even though this may mean a loss of revenue from trees in the short-term.

WHAT IS ECOTOURISM?

Tourists bring economic benefits to communities when they travel to natural places to see and experience the wilderness. No one travels to see a clear-cut! When visitors bring revenue to a community, locals begin to see the natural environment as having value, which can be incentive to look after and preserve wild places. If enough jobs are created through ecotourism, there's more motivation to protect natural resources and manage them in a **sustainable** way. Ecotourism, though, must be carefully managed. Too many people visiting a sensitive natural area can damage the environment we are trying to protect.

Ecotourism has made a big difference in the local economies of Rwanda, Uganda and the Democratic Republic of Congo, where governments have capitalized on the world's interest in saving the critically endangered mountain gorilla. Mountain gorillas are found only in a couple of protected rainforest areas in the Congo Basin. Visitors come from all over the world for a chance to see these great apes in their natural environment. The result is that this endangered population is slowly increasing, and its forest home is being protected.

WHAT IS AGROFORESTRY?

Landowners don't need to choose either forestry *or* farming. Agroforestry combines both land uses in the same place. Animals graze under trees, or trees and shrubs are planted beside crops. In Yanamono, Peru, an agroforestry project that allows animals to graze among the trees has the added benefit of introducing animal manure as a form of natural fertilizer.

Stop Talking, Start Planting

If you feel frustrated by how much time adults spend talking about deforestation without taking action, you will understand why Felix Finkbeiner from Germany started Plant-for-the-Planet.

Inspired by such people as Richard St. Barbe Baker and Kenyan activist Wangari Maathai, Finkbeiner suggested that children plant one million trees in every country on Earth. He began his project in 2007, at age nine, and within three years children in Germany had accomplished that goal.

Today children in the organization teach and inspire other children about the benefits of planting trees. The goal now is to plant one trillion trees all over the world. If you're interested in becoming one of the child ambassadors for the project, visit the Plant-for-the-Planet website for more details.

The practice of silvopasture provides grazing for livestock without first clearing the land of trees.
COURTESY OF USDA NATURAL RESOURCES CONSERVATION SERVICE

The cups on the trunks of these trees in Thailand are used to collect rubber.

THIDARAT PETPRASOM/DREAMSTIME.COM

SHH! TREES AT WORK!

Some forest-based industries harvest products from trees without destroying the forest.

Most of us are familiar with the idea of wood being used as a fuel source. A wood-burning fire, though, is not necessarily the most efficient way to convert the carbon stored in tree fibers into heat energy.

Some trees, like the babassu palm, which grows in the Amazon, produce a type of vegetable oil that can be burned and used as fuel for light, cooking and heat. A group of 500 trees can produce up to 125 barrels of oil each year.

NEW FOOD SOURCES

Our taste buds are used to a modest selection of food when you consider that there are about 75,000 plants that have some edible part. Did you know, for example, that there are 5,000 varieties of potatoes? And yet in the grocery store we see the same few types available all the time.

Many potential sources of food grow in rainforests and could be cultivated in a way that does not destroy the surrounding forest. We don't know what the superfoods of the future may be. Without the reservoir of plant species that remain in our rainforests, we may never know what tasty and nutritious powerhouse we are missing out on.

BUILD UP, NOT OUT

This building in Milan, Italy, is a great example of using vertical space to grow a veritable forest of greenery.

VICTOR/UNSPLASH.COM

One of the reasons forests are cut down is to make room for cities to expand. Building taller skyscrapers within the limits of existing cities rather than spreading out is one way to reduce urban sprawl.

CLONING FOR THE FUTURE

David Milarch from Michigan is on a mission to gather DNA from the largest, finest and oldest trees in the world. The Archangel Ancient Tree Archive collects cuttings from old trees around the world and clones these beautiful specimens. The clones are used to establish new forests using ancient genetics. By nurturing young versions of old trees, the foundation is creating a living archive of genetics that would otherwise be lost should something happen to the last remaining old-growth trees.

Cloning ancient trees is one way to preserve genetics that might otherwise be lost when old giants die.
ARCHANGEL ANCIENT TREE ARCHIVE

MAKING CHANGES

While I was researching and writing this book, I found myself alternating between feeling sad about the forests we have lost and hopeful about changes in attitudes and understanding about the many ways forests help keep us all healthy.

There are many things each of us can do to stop wasting forest resources. Choosing recycled paper products, trying to avoid too much cardboard packaging, looking for the rainforest-friendly logo, conserving electricity by turning off lights and lowering the thermostat are just a few of the ways we can look after our forests every day. I've also decided to support a couple of the nonprofit organizations that have tree-planting projects.

If each of us contributes in some way, together we can help preserve some of the stunning forests that make our planet so beautiful and use more wisely the trees we do decide to harvest.

Students, soldiers and villagers work together on a reforestation project in Thailand. SOMRERK WITTHAYANANT/SHUTTERSTOCK.COM

Resources

Print

Baker, Lucy. *Life in the Rain Forests (World Book Ecology series).* Chicago, IL: World Book Inc., 2001.

Beresford-Kroeger, Diana. *The Global Forest: 40 Ways Trees Can Save Us.* New York, NY: Penguin Random House, 2011.

Colson, Mary. *Unstable Earth: What Happens If the Rainforests Disappear?* Mankato, MN: A+, Smart Apple Media, 2015.

Hammond, Herb. *Seeing the Forest Among the Trees: The Case for Holistic Forest Use.* Vancouver, BC: Polestar Publishing, 1992.

Hellum, A.K. *Listening to Trees.* Edmonton, AB: NeWest Press, 2008.

Moore, Patrick. *Green Spirit: Trees Are the Answer.* Vancouver, BC: Greenspirit Enterprises, 2000.

Parry, James. *Rainforest Safari.* London, UK: Carlton Books, 2008.

Vandermeer, John, and Ivette Perfecto. *Breakfast of Biodiversity: The Political Ecology of Rain Forest Destruction.* Oakland, CA: Food First Books, 2005.

Online

Arbor Day: ArborDay.org
Archangel Ancient Tree Archive: ancienttreearchive.org
Canadian Institute of Forestry (History): cif-ifc.org/forest-history
Center for International Forestry Research: cifor.org
Climate Institute: climate.org/deforestation-and-climate-change
Collaborative Partnership on Forests: cpfweb.org/en
Discovering Forests Learning Guide: fao.org/3/a-i6207e.pdf
Great Bear Rainforest: greatbearrainforest.gov.bc.ca
Great Green Wall: greatgreenwall.org/about-great-green-wall
Mongabay Tropical Rainforest Information for Kids: kids.mongabay.com
National Geographic Kids: kids.nationalgeographic.com
Palm Oil Scorecard: palmoilscorecard.panda.org
Plant-for-the-Planet: plant-for-the-planet.org/en/home
Rainforest Alliance: rainforest-alliance.org

Glossary

afforestation—the process of creating a forest, particularly in an area where no trees grew previously

biodiversity—the presence of many different kinds of plants and animals in an environment

carbon sink—an environment able to absorb and store atmospheric carbon dioxide

civil disobedience—deliberate defiance of the law as a way to put pressure on a government to change legislation

conifer—a type of tree that's usually evergreen, with narrow, needle-shaped leaves

cutblock—a specific area in which tree harvesting is permitted

deforestation—the permanent clearing of a large area of trees

ecosystem—an environment in which plants and animals form an interrelated and complete community

elevation—the height of a point of land above sea level

erosion—the gradual wearing away of soil or rock as a result of natural forces like wind and water

fungi—a group of living organisms that includes mushrooms, molds, yeasts and mildews

groundwater—fresh water that is stored underground rather than on the surface of the earth in streams, rivers or lakes

Indigenous People—a population that originates from or occupies a particular region and has deep relationships with the land and environment

infrastructure—the basic buildings and structures (roads, sewers, power grids) needed for a country (or region) to function properly

native species—a species that has historically lived and thrived in a particular ecosystem

old-growth forest—an ancient forest that has been allowed to grow and develop with little or no outside interference

photosynthesis—the process by which plants convert sunlight into nutrients needed to sustain life

raw logs—unprocessed logs that have not yet been used for lumber or pulp and paper products

sustainable—a way of harvesting or using a resource without depleting the available supply

water cycle—circulation of Earth's water through evaporation, condensation and precipitation

Index

Index (continued)